A PORT THROUGH TIME

ILLUSTRATED BY STEVE NOON

WRITTEN BY DR. ANNE MILLARD

London, New York, Melbourne,
Munich, and Delhi

Project Editor Jenny Finch
Art Editor Sheila Collins
Senior Editor Francesca Baines
Managing Editor Linda Esposito
Managing Art Editor Diane Thistlethwaite
Publishing Manager Andrew Macintyre
Category Publisher Laura Buller
Picture Researcher Myriam Megharbi, Rob Nunn
DK Picture Researcher Rose Horridge, Claire Bowers
Production Controller Seyhan Esen-Yagmurlu
DTP Designer Siu Chan

This edition published in the United States in 2006
by DK Publishing, Inc.
375 Hudson Street
New York, New York 10014

06 07 08 09 10 10 9 8 7 6 5 4 3 2 1

A catalog record for this book is available
from the Library of Congress

ISBN-13: 978-0-75662-221-3
ISBN-10: 0-7566-2221-2

Color reproduction by Wyndeham-Icon, UK
Printed and bound by Tien Wah Press, Malaysia

Discover more at
www.dk.com

CONTENTS

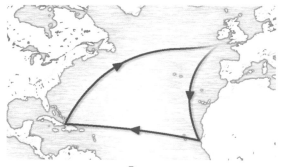

THE STORY OF A PORT

About 10,000 years ago, the Ice Age ended and new plants and animals spread across Europe, followed by human beings who quickly adapted to the warmer conditions. Our story is set on the coast, along the sheltered shores of a large natural bay, and explains why this special place developed over time into a thriving port. It focuses on the different ships and goods that passed through the port and the trading links forged with peoples and places all around the world. The story follows the fortunes of the port and the people who lived here, through good times and bad, and shows how it changed through history as needs, tastes, and opportunities altered.

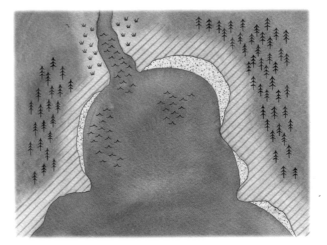

AERIAL VIEW OF THE BAY

KEY

WOODLAND   BEACH

FIRM GROUND   MARSHLAND

NATURAL HARBOR

The water is shallow along the shoreline, but it is very deep further out in the bay. Marshes spread around the river mouth and many birds live in its reeds. The land slopes up from the shore, and on this higher ground a thick forest grows, which is home to many animals and birds.

STONE-AGE HUNTERS (AROUND 9,000 YEARS AGO)

Every summer, a tribe of hunter-gatherers camps on the shores of the bay. It is a good spot, sheltered from any storms. There is fresh water to drink and birds and their eggs to eat. The tribespeople hunt game and gather plants and berries in the forest. They fish from canoes made of hollowed-out tree trunks and gather shellfish. In winter, they move inland and trade highly prized shells for other goods from the tribes they meet there.

EARLY FARMERS (AROUND 5,000 YEARS AGO)

When knowledge of farming spread across Europe, a tribe settled by the bay where their ancestors had camped. Besides raising crops and animals, they still do some hunting and a lot of fishing. Representatives of a tribe from farther inland sail down the river bringing top-quality flints from their mine to trade for dried fish, reed baskets, and other goods. Others from a third tribe living a long way down the coast come by boat to join the trading.

BRONZE-AGE JEWELRY

Archeologists have found examples of skillfully crafted jewelry—such as these gold bracelets—made by smiths in the Bronze Age.

IRON-AGE FLAGON

As well as practical tools and weapons, iron-age smiths made objects of great beauty. This bronze flagon, decorated with coral, was used for pouring wine, beer, or mead at feasts. It would have been a valuable trade item.

IRON AGE (AROUND 2,300 YEARS AGO)

People have discovered how to work iron, which is much harder than bronze. Some goods are traded right across Europe over land, by rivers, and along the coasts. The bay is popular because it provides sheltered moorings. The villagers have built a quay made of rubble enclosed in wood, where larger ships can moor. Occasionally, they are even visited by adventurers from the Mediterranean world who exchange wine and luxury goods for furs, amber, cloth, slaves, and any metals the villagers will sell.

BRONZE AGE (AROUND 3,500 YEARS AGO)

People have discovered how to work gold and how to make bronze from copper and tin. The village has two highly skilled metal smiths—a father and son. Traders come long distances to buy their tools, weapons, and jewels. Increased trade makes the village and its chief rich and respected. They now control land right around the bay. Our villagers also travel long distances to buy tin and special hard stones that make querns, used to grind grain. They also mount expeditions to quarry large slabs of stone to build monuments honoring their gods and goddesses and their dead ancestors.

WHERE IS HE?

This is a very unlucky and accident-prone man—and so are all his descendants. Trace the disasters that befall them through the centuries. They are easy to spot because they are all dressed in red, yellow, and green. To check you've found them turn to page 32.

UNDER ROMAN RULE (C. 150 C.E.)

The Romans have conquered the port, bringing with them Roman laws and customs. The port is governed from the Basilica, which also houses the law courts, and people worship Roman gods and goddesses. Many foreigners have settled here, and exotic goods are imported from distant parts of the Roman Empire. In turn, local goods are exported, including grain, wool, silver, slaves, and even bears and wolves destined for the arena in Rome.

Can you see who has stepped in elephant dung?

Marble is imported from Italy to decorate important buildings.

Temple

Greek teacher

Public speaker

Basilica

Forum (market)

Cloth merchant

Papyrus store

Apartments

Apartments

Slaves escaping

Glassware

Jeweler

Greek doctor

Ivory

Merchant's house

Spices

Olive oil

Shrine

Furs

Olives

Wolf

Bear

Wine

Litter

Syrian merchant

Wool for export

6

Missionary

Merchant

Celts

Local traders have brought salt from along the coast to sell at the market.

Lions and other wild beasts are imported to entertain the crowds in the local arena.

Slaves about to be sent to Rome try to escape from their guards.

Find the clumsy slave who is getting a beating.

Arena

Metal smith

Workshops

Soldiers

Boat building

Fishermen's nets

Potter

Washing clothes

Warehouses

Spanish horses

Trading ship

Spanish lawyer

Grain

Timber

Patrolling the coast

Bronze worker

Grain for export

Guarding silver

Treadmill crane

Pottery

vern

Escaping lion

Silk

Jars of fish condiment

Spices

Ship carrying exports

Local fishermen

Furs

Salt

Grain

7

Port officials keep a record of all imports and exports so they can be taxed.

This ship has brought expensive treasures from the East, such as silk and spices.

A New Start (c. 950)

Many foreign invaders have settled in the port and mixed with the local people. Christianity, which became the official religion of the late Roman period, has survived the fall of the Roman Empire. The Church is becoming rich and powerful. A lord governs the area for the king, and a chief runs the port's day-to-day affairs. The lord charges the people taxes in return for protection against Viking raiders and hostile neighboring lords. Most trade is local, though some exotic goods are imported for the very rich. The main exports are grain, fish, honey, furs, wool, and salt.

Wedding party ship

Fishing

Imported ivory and wine

Jetty

Pilgrims

Wool

Dyeing cloth

Drying fish

Making barrels

Sail

Thatchers

Cloth

Baskets

Toilet

Leather wares

Bead maker

Jewelry

Dried foods

Grinding grain

Salting fish

Honey

Ivory and bone

Fish

Fisherwomen

Glass beads

Grain

Apple thief!

8

Spot the antlers about to be made into a comb.

Fish is caught, preserved, and then exported to neighboring towns.

Some Vikings are peaceful and have come to trade exotic goods brought from the East.

Captives from local feuds and Viking raids are sold as slaves at the market.

Christian missionaries are setting off to convert pagans abroad.

How many ruined Roman buildings can you see?

Fort

Defensive wall

Boat building

Viking trader

Smith

Warship guarding the coast

Chief's hall

Merchant's ship

Tannery

Falcons

Wine and grain

Salt making

Pottery

Store

Carpenter

Stained glass window

Wine

Drying fish

Loom

Scales

Slave market

Furs

Iron weapons

Spinning

Glass

Silk

Furs

Axe heads

Bronze

Church

Quernstones

Wool

Priest

Local merchant

Missionaries

9

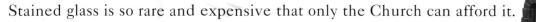 Stained glass is so rare and expensive that only the Church can afford it.

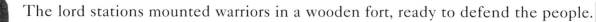 The lord stations mounted warriors in a wooden fort, ready to defend the people.

WIDENING HORIZONS (C. 1190)

It is the morning of the weekly market, and people have come from the surrounding countryside to sell their produce. The port is ruled by a lord, but the merchants and craftsmen have started to form guilds and become more powerful. Religious wars, called Crusades, are being fought in the Middle East, bringing people into contact with exotic goods like sugar and spices. The Italian ports of Venice and Genoa control the trade in these goods, which are very expensive. Most trade is local, with grain, fur, honey, and wool exported to neighbouring countries.

Boats for coastal and river trade

Tannery

Dyeing cloth

Wheelwright

Smithy

Harness maker

Sharpening tools

Logs

Carpenter's workshop

Leather worker

Stained glass windows

Tapestry

Candlemakers

Moneylender   Anxious clients

Washerwoman

Store

Grain

Crusaders

Priest

Crusaders' soldiers

Stave fight

Stocks

Dancing bear

Ribbons

Drinking water for sale

Animals for sale

Honey

Furs

Wealthy pilgrims

Pilgrims

10

What has made the pigs stampede?

Christian Crusaders are off to win back the Holy Land from the Muslim Saracens.

Venetian ship

Silk

Pepper

Raisins

Ivory

Barrel-maker

Potter

Kilns

Loading Crusaders' horses

Loading wool for export

Loading Crusaders' supplies

Crusaders' ship

Merchant's house

Stone

Bathhouse

Baker

Bailiff's house

Weaver's house

Packing wool

Toilet

Inn

Inn's stables

Drunken brawl

Hardware and iron dealer

Lady's coach

Merchant

Beggar

Baskets

Cheese

Packhorses

Pottery

Fleeces

Fish

Eggs

Vegetables

Bread

Birds

Bone

Cloth

Fish

11

Local farmers have brought vegetables to sell at the market. Find the nobleman who has just been hit by a ball.

FUN OF THE FAIR (C. 1450)

The lord has sold a charter for the port, and it is now run by the mayor and a council made up of rich merchants and guild masters. They hold an annual fair, and foreign merchants from across Europe flock to buy and sell. For local people, it is very profitable—and great fun! Italians still control trade with the East, and have invented banking, opening branches all over Europe.

How many traveling performers can you spot at the fair?

For a fee, ship owners will carry other traders' goods.

Lord's castle

Guildhall

Shops

Boat building

Timber

Scandinavian ship

Flemish ship

Venetian ship

Crane

Venetian merchant galley

Italian armor

Tar

German ship

French wine

Local grain

Venetian ship

Loading goods for river trade

Bringing goods ashore

Maps

Sailors

Traveling dentist

Sick sailor

Piper

Ferryman

Portuguese ship

Spanish swords

Dancer

Clerk

Grain

Cannon

Local cheeses

Spinning tops

Fire-eater

Cockfight

Pickpoc

12

Warlike Turks—who now rule the Middle East and North Africa—are rare visitors.

An Italian from the port's bank changes foreign coins and arranges loans.

Murderers are punished by hanging, then tarred and displayed as a warning.

Find the fuel people have started using.

Church

Windmill

Gatehouse

Warehouses

Portcullis

Executed criminal

Coal barge

Grain

Preaching friar

Acrobats

English cloth

Swedish furs

Flemish tapestries

Juggler on stilts

Grain

Hay cart

Clerk

Silk

Mugger

Sugar loaves

Medicines

Officials

Hat stand

Spanish leather

Puppet show

Perfume

Burgundians buying wool

Exotic fruits

Italian banker

Ale

Salt

Wine

Tailor

Spices

Hawks

Turks

African slave

Beggar

Exotic fruits

Peddler

Performing monkey

Roasting spit

Wrestling competition

Pies

Herald

Foreign merchants

13

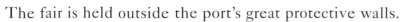

NEW WORLDS, NEW GOODS (C. 1590)

The Christian Church has split into Catholics and Protestants. They are bitter enemies. Catholic Spain has claimed the New World (the Americas) for its empire, forbidding others (even Catholic countries) to trade there. Ships ignore the ban, bringing back strange people, animals, and plants. In the guildhall, officials greet explorers who are displaying treasures looted from a Spanish galleon.

Can you see Barbary pirates seizing people as slaves?

High-ranking Native Americans have come on a goodwill visit.

Labels in illustration: Map-maker · Guildhall · Pipe · Mayor and wife · Merchant's house · Emptying chamber pot · Glass window · Spices · Turkeys · Native Americans · Stores · Native American · Goods unloaded from ships · Coal cart · Pillory · Flower seller · Water seller · Welcome home · Trying tobacco · Strange plant · Port official · Cocoa beans · Welcome home · Parrot · Captured treasure · Trying a potato

Church

Warehouses

Gunpowder

Hauling
up goods

Russian
furs

Shops

Pirates

Pirates' galley

Goose girl

Navigation
lesson

Salt cod from
Newfoundland

Silk

Spy

Unloading
cloth

Venetian
ship

Port officials

Captain's family

Captain's
cabin

Fire in
the galley

Spices
and silk

Large ransoms will be paid for Spanish nobles captured at sea.

Can you see a pickpocket and his victim on the quay?

15

 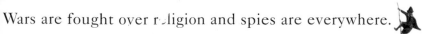

New Wealth, Old Problems (c. 1630)

New riches flow into the port from direct trade with the East and from the new slave trade—a triangular arrangement whereby goods are exported to West Africa in exchange for slaves, who are transported to the New World (the Americas). Shipbuilding and repairs are also profitable. Across Europe, wars between Catholics and Protestants are still raging, and some people are leaving to settle colonies in the New World to escape religious persecution.

Carpenter's workshop

Blacksmith

Norwegian timber

Raising mast

Workshop

Carpenter

Scaffold

Shipbuilding

Shipwright

Strict Protestants

Children playing

Oysters

Pedlar

Cannons

Bank

Inn

Customs house

Paying import duty

Store of duty goods

Rope-maker

Ship repairing

Sealing ship's hull with tar

16

The telescope is a new invention that is useful to both astronomers and sailors.

How are ships' hulls made watertight?

New-World mahogany and rosewood are in demand for the best furniture.

How do sailors on the slave ship spend their spare time?

Slaves are forced to exercise by dancing to the beat of a drum.

Furling the sail

Dead slave

Exercising slaves

Drummer

Anchor

Gambling

Sea sick!

Lantern

Captain

Crew's quarters

Helmsman

Feeding

Captain's slave

Slave ship

18

 Sails have to be furled (rolled up) and let down by hand.

 The helmsman steers the ship using the whipstaff – a long vertical pole attached to the rudder.

Pirate ship

Firing cannons

Lookout

Dining room

Officers' bunks

Cannonball splashing in the sea

Arms store

Stores

Porcelain

Coffee

Silk

Spices

Ship from the East

PIRATES AND PROFITS (C. 1690)

In the Atlantic Ocean off the coast of Africa, a slave ship is taking its human cargo to the New World to sell to plantation owners. The profits will buy goods from the sugar and tobacco plantations to sell in Europe. Another merchant ship is heading back to our port, laden with luxury goods from the East that will bring vast profits—as long as pirates don't get to them first!

THE PRICE OF PROFIT (C. 1770)

Increased trade and the growth of colonies in the East and the New World have made some merchants and nobles very wealthy. But for most people life is hard, and many turn to crime. The government imposes high taxes on imported goods to pay for wars over frontiers and colonies, so smuggling is widespread. Men must be careful at night or they will be kidnapped by the press gang and forced to join the Navy.

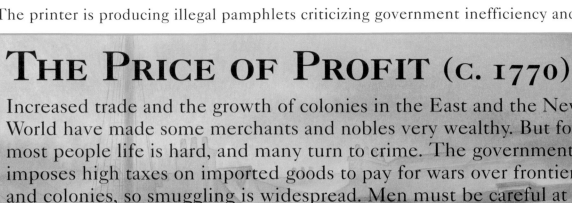

Coffee stores

Servant's room

Scientist

Rich merchant

Drinking tea

Coffee house

Insurance office

Coffee brewing

Printer

Drunken sailors

Sedan chair

Muggers

Night watchmen

Mahogany from the Americas

Smugglers

20

Find the sailor who is jumping ship.

Night watchmen are badly paid and won't risk their own lives to help others.

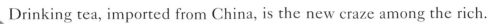

Highwayman

Fence

Gambling dispute

Boxing match

Theater

Guard

Chinese porcelain

Imported antiques

Tavern

Corrupt clergyman

Muslin and cotton from India

Clearing waste from privies

Press gang

Pack ponies

Wounded sailor

Landlord

Thieves

Captain's cabin

Tattooing

Customs officer

Jumping ship

Soldiers

Brandy

Smugglers

Muffled hooves

In Europe, freed slaves like this barmaid find poorly paid work. How many men are hiding from the press gang?

21

INDUSTRY AND EMPIRE (c. 1890)

The port has been transformed by the Industrial Revolution—goods are now produced by the use of machines in factories. This dramatic change is the result of inventions such as the steam engine, which can power machines, trains, and ships. People from the countryside have flocked into the port to work, and living and working conditions are appalling. Abroad, the country's empire has grown to include parts of Africa. Raw materials from the colonies are imported and the manufactured goods made with them are exported back again.

Iron

Chemical fertilizer

Clipper ship

Telegraph office　Emigrants

Lifeboat

First-class lounge · Second class

First class

Third-class bunks

Mail sacks

For the zoo

Police　Jewish refugees

African chiefs

Port officials' boat

Coal barge

Colonial civil servants

Band

Stowaway

Explorers bound for Africa

Diplomats from the East

Paddleboat taking passengers to the liner

Photographer

Air pump

Diver recovering lost goods

Dockers

Passenger liner from the East

22

Some longshoremen have gone on strike. They want better pay and conditions. Refrigerated ships bring fresh produce, such as meat, from across the world.

New, cheap cigarettes are proving very popular. Can you see two new methods of long-distance communication?

Imported cotton

Imported tobacco

Timber

Steam engine

Cloth for export

Tea chests

Steam tug

Passenger liner bound for Africa

Paper

Grain

Warehouse

Telephone

Soldiers off to the colonies

Messenger boy

Diamonds

Gold

Strikers

Wine

Merchant

Gas streetlight

Ship repairs

Rat catchers

Officials

Frozen meat

Newsboy

Smoking

Women packers

Steam crane

Coffee

Ivory for billiard balls

23

Vulcanized (chemically treated) rubber is used in many new inventions, such as bicycle tires. Inexpensive wheat from America is causing local farmers problems.

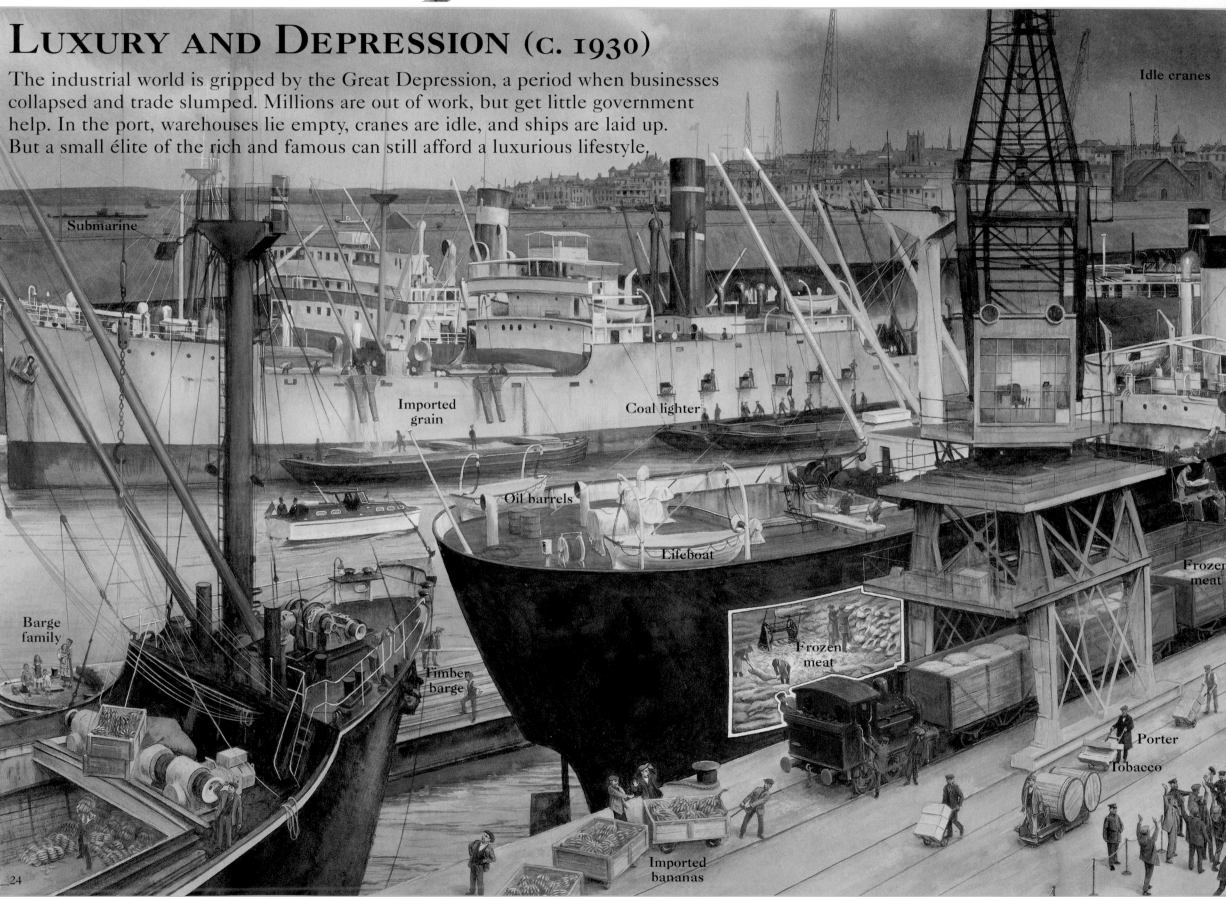

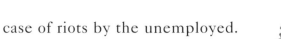

Soldiers stand by in case of riots by the unemployed.   Even in the depression the arms trade thrives, as European countries stockpile weapons for future conflicts.

LUXURY AND DEPRESSION (C. 1930)

The industrial world is gripped by the Great Depression, a period when businesses collapsed and trade slumped. Millions are out of work, but get little government help. In the port, warehouses lie empty, cranes are idle, and ships are laid up. But a small élite of the rich and famous can still afford a luxurious lifestyle.

Idle cranes

Submarine

Imported grain

Coal lighter

Oil barrels

Lifeboat

Frozen meat

Barge family

Frozen meat

Timber barge

Porter

Tobacco

Imported bananas

Who has been given a shock by an unexpected import?

Cars are mass-produced on assembly lines, lowering their price.

24

Women are paid less, so these typists still have jobs in the shipping office.

Planes cross the Atlantic, but flights are hugely expensive and considered risky.

Movies are very popular, so visiting stars cause a stir.

Who is earning a living entertaining the crowds on the quayside?

Airplane

Oil depot

Radio room

Oil sheikhs

Seasick

Warships

Tanks for export

Tobacco

Sugar

Soldiers

Gangster and bodyguards

Italian count

American millionairess

Radio reporter

Maid

Reporters

Customs men

Movie stars

Police

Typists

Manager

Movie mogul

Street entertainer

Foreman

Soup kitchen

Bellboy

Wine supplies

Luggage

Secretary

Unemployed longshoremen

25

The new radio provides news, education, and entertainment to a growing audience.

World War I (1914–1918) saw more women working, and now many have careers.

BUSINESS AND PLEASURE (PRESENT DAY)

Multinational companies now control the majority of the port's trade, and container shipping has streamlined the transportation of goods. The port has a new marina and many new leisure facilities, because ordinary people have more time and money to enjoy themselves. People are also more environmentally aware, and campaign to protect wildlife and historic buildings.

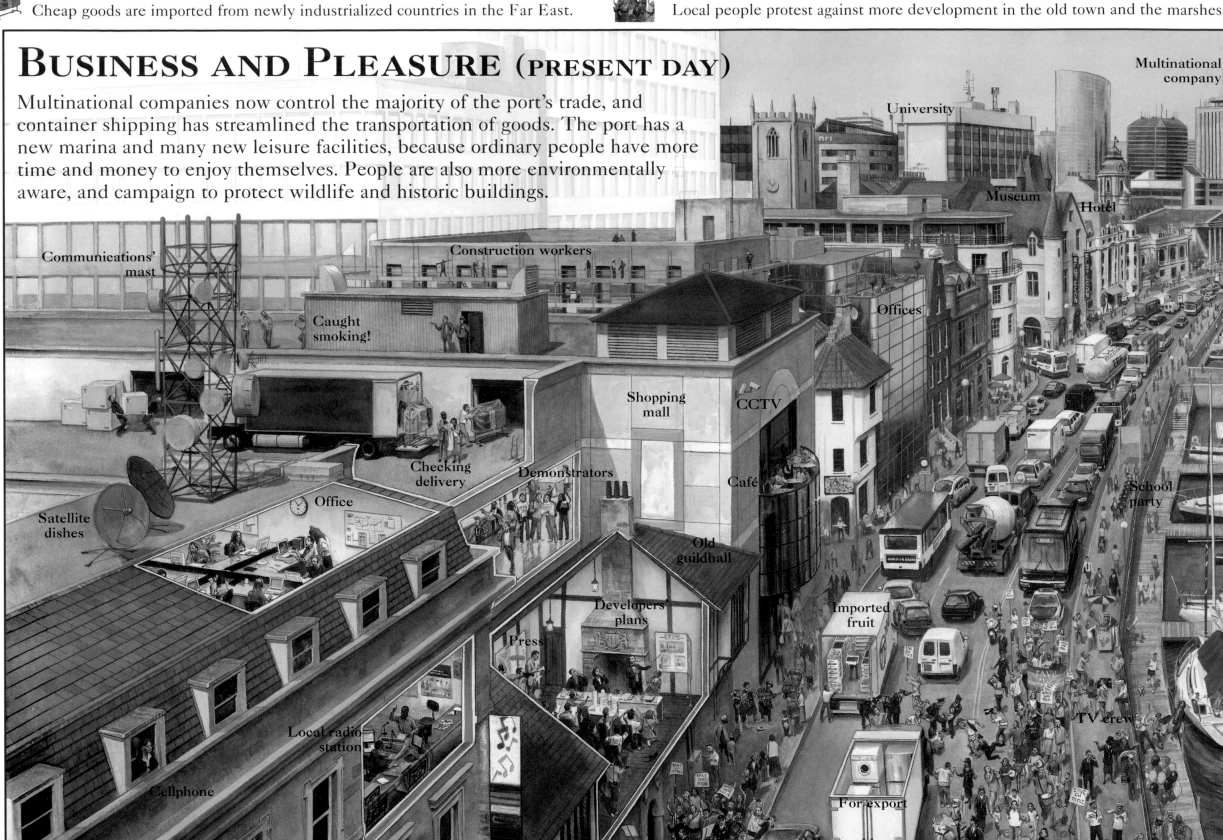

How many new ways to communicate can you spot?

Old warehouses have been converted into a shopping mall.

Multinational company

University

Museum

Hotel

Communications' mast

Construction workers

Caught smoking!

Offices

Shopping mall

CCTV

Satellite dishes

Office

Checking delivery

Demonstrators

Café

School party

Old guildhall

Developers' plans

Imported fruit

Press

Local radio station

Cellphone

For export

TV crew

Texting

Demonstrators

Air-sea rescue
helicopter

Grain silos

Oil refinery

Nature
reserve

Cruise
liner

Luxury
apartments

Container
ship

Satellite
navigation

Computerized
bridge

Visiting foreign
warship

Captain

Cabin

Using a
laptop

Fishermen's
boats

Jacuzzi

Dining
room

Ferry

Jet-skis

Marina

Luxury yacht

Smugglers

Customs'
launch

Illegal
immigrant

Immigration
officers

Sniffer
dog

27

A World of Trade

Over the centuries, traders have often proved to be explorers, discovering new lands as well as new goods. Trade went on to shape the world, as new ports were established, existing ports grew, and some countries were colonized.

ALEXANDRIA   This Egyptian city was founded in 332 B.C.E. by Alexander the Great. It grew into a center of learning and trade, and became one of the great cities of his empire. Around 299 B.C.E., work began on a huge lighthouse just outside the busy port. Called the Pharos, the lighthouse was one of the Seven Wonders of the World.

AMSTERDAM   The capital of Holland was at its height during the 17th and 18th centuries when the country was a great sea power, and the Dutch East India Company controlled trade with the East Indies and South Africa. Starting in the 16th century to the present day, Amsterdam has been a center for the diamond trade.

ARCHANGEL   Until 1703, the only Russian trading port was Archangel on the Arctic coast. Although icebound half the year, icebreakers now make access possible and it is a busy port today. Major exports are wood and timber products.

BORDEAUX   One of the most valuable commodities in the medieval period was wine. France was a major wine producer and the port of Bordeaux, on the Atlantic coast, was the chief exporting city.

MAP SHOWING SOME OF THE KEY PORTS OF THE WORLD

CADIZ   Situated on a headland, there has been a port on the Atlantic coast of Spain at Cadiz since 1100 B.C.. In the 16th century, Cadiz became the base for Spanish treasure ships during the conquest of the New World.

CAPE TOWN   On the southwestern tip of South Africa, Cape Town was founded in 1652 as a supply station for the Dutch East India Company. It is still an important port today, exporting gold, diamonds, and fruit.

PRECIOUS SPICES

For thousands of years spices have been highly prized. Once cinnamon was more valuable than gold, and pepper so precious it was used as money. Spices became important in Europe in the Middle Ages for flavoring meat that had been preserved in salt. The huge profits to be made from the spice trade drove European merchants west to find new routes to India.

GDANSK   The Polish port of Gdansk lies on the Baltic Sea and was formerly known as Danzig. The port joined the Hanseatic League in the 13th century, which was an alliance of trading cities around the Baltic that became the most important economic power in the medieval period.

GENOA   The city of Genoa in Italy prospered under Roman rule, and again during the Crusades, as soldiers and traders passed through the port on the way to and from the Holy Land. It went on to become a powerful trade and banking center, and today Genoa is Italy's chief port.

HONG KONG   Hong Kong Island, on the southeast coast of China, became a British colony in the mid-19th century and was occupied under an arrangement that ended in 1997, when it was returned to China. Its position, on the edge of China, has made the port an important center of trade and banking between the East and West.

ISTANBUL   The Turkish port of Istanbul lies on a channel, called the Bosporus, that links the Mediterranean Sea to the Black Sea and Asia beyond. It was founded in 660 B.C.E. as Byzantium, and in 330 C.E. was renamed Constantinople when it became the capital of the Eastern Roman Empire. The port's rich history and position on the edge of two continents gives it an exciting and exotic mix of peoples and cultures.

JAKARTA   On the island of Java, Jakarta is the largest city in Indonesia. It was founded in 1691 by the Dutch and was at that time called Batavia. It was the center of trade for spices, such as nutmeg, cinnamon, cloves, and pepper, as well as tea, silk, and Chinese porcelain.

JEDDA   Jedda, or Jidda, lies on the Red Sea in Saudi Arabia. For hundreds of years, it has been a key port for Muslims from all over the world making the pilgrimage, or hajj, to Mecca.

KOZHIKODE Until the 19th century, Calicut, now called Kozhikode, was the main port of southern India. It first became a center for trade with Arab merchants, and later with merchants from Europe. It is now important for trade in timber, coconuts, spices, tea, and coffee.

GOLD ORE

GOLDRUSH
Until gold was discovered nearby in 1848, San Francisco was just a small town on the West Coast of America. With the arrival of thousands of fortune hunters, it quickly grew into a bustling port. A few years later, the discovery of gold in Australia led to the boom of the ports of Melbourne and Perth.

LISBON The Portuguese capital has been an important trading center for thousands of years. In the 15th century, explorers set off from Lisbon in search of India. In 1731, a terrible earthquake almost completely destroyed the city.

MARSEILLES The oldest city in France, Marseilles was settled by Greeks from the East around 660 B.C.E.. The port lies on the Mediterranean Sea, and during the Crusades became a centre of trade as many pilgrims and soldiers passed through on their way to the Holy Land. Today, Marseilles is one of France's most important seaports and a major industrial city.

MUMBAI The main port and industrial center of India is Mumbai, on the Arabian Sea. It lies on seven islands around a natural deep-water harbor. In the 16th century, Portugal controlled this area of India and the city was known as Bombay, Portuguese for "good bay." But from the 17th century, until Indian independence in 1947, it was controlled by Britain.

NEW YORK Founded by the Dutch in 1624 as New Amsterdam, New York was renamed by the British in 1664. It lies on the East Coast of the USA. In the 18th century, it became a center for banking and the Stock Exchange, and by 1840 New York had become the leading port in the USA. In the 19th century, huge numbers of immigrants from Europe passed through the port on their way to seek their fortune in America.

OSTIA This ancient Italian city, at the mouth of the Tiber River, was the port of the Roman capital. It was at its height of activity in the first century C.E., as goods from all over the Roman Empire passed through the port.

PANAMA CANAL The Panama canal links the Pacific and Atlantic Oceans. It was opened in 1914 and is 51 miles (82 km) long. Its construction meant ships could avoid the dangerous waters off Cape Horn, at the tip of South America, and halved the journey between San Francisco and New York from 14,000 miles (22,500 km) to 6,000 miles (9,500 km).

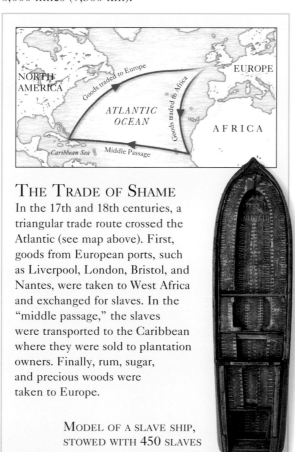

THE TRADE OF SHAME
In the 17th and 18th centuries, a triangular trade route crossed the Atlantic (see map above). First, goods from European ports, such as Liverpool, London, Bristol, and Nantes, were taken to West Africa and exchanged for slaves. In the "middle passage," the slaves were transported to the Caribbean where they were sold to plantation owners. Finally, rum, sugar, and precious woods were taken to Europe.

MODEL OF A SLAVE SHIP, STOWED WITH 450 SLAVES

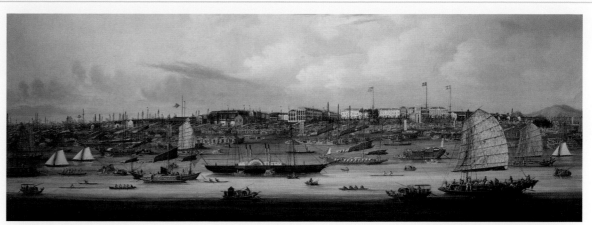

THE TEA TRADE
Until the middle of the 19th century, China was closed to trade with the outside world. One of the first ports to trade regularly with Europe was Canton (now Guangzhou), and it soon became the capital of China's tea trade with Europe. This painting shows the Pearl River in Canton, busy with local junks and the Hong Kong steamship.

BUNDLES OF TEA

PIRAEUS The largest port in Greece is Piraeus, the port of Athens. It was built in the 5th century B.C.E. around a natural deep harbor, and was fortified with walls to protect the Athenian fleet. But in 396 C.E. the port was destroyed and abandoned until the 19th century, when Athens became the Greek capital.

QUEBEC One of the first European settlements in Canada, Quebec became the center of the fur trade. Colonized by the French in 1608, the French and English fought over Quebec many times. Today, it is the heart of French Canada.

ROTTERDAM The largest port in Europe and one of the most modern in the world, Rotterdam is situated at the mouth of the Rhine River in Holland. It is linked to the sea by a canal large enough for ocean-going ships.

SINGAPORE The port of Singapore, in southeastern Asia, has been a trading center since the 14th century. In the 19th century Singapore was controlled by the British and the East India Company. It grew rapidly as trade developed with merchants from Malaysia and China. Today, Singapore is one of the biggest ports in the world and a major international financial center.

ST. PETERSBURG St. Petersburg was founded in 1703 by the Russian czar, Peter the Great. He built it as a naval base and a port for trade in the Baltic. It soon became an industrial and cultural center and Russia's leading seaport.

SUEZ CANAL The Suez Canal in Egypt links the Mediterranean Sea with the Red Sea and the Indian Ocean. It is 100 miles (160 km) long and took 10 years to build. It was opened in 1869 and made a huge impact on world trade, cutting the distance between London and Bombay (now Mumbai) by 4,425 miles (7,125 km).

VENICE Venice lies on a network of canals and lagoons in northeastern Italy. It became a trading city between the 9th and 11th centuries and soon dominated the eastern Mediterranean Sea. By the 13th century it had become a great sea power, together with the rival city of Genoa on the other side of Italy. Its power declined in the 15th century with the discovery of America and sea routes to Asia.

YOKOHAMA The port of Yokohama in Japan only opened up to trade with foreign countries in 1859. It became the center for trade with Japan, and was famous for the export of silk.

SHIPPING THROUGH THE AGES

The story of ships began thousands of years ago, when people realized that they could cross water using a log. Rafts and dugout canoes with paddles followed, then boats of wooden planks, and the use of oars. Next sails were used, at first only when the wind was blowing in the right direction, but then a zig-zagging technique, called tacking, was discovered, and sails could be used wherever the wind blew.

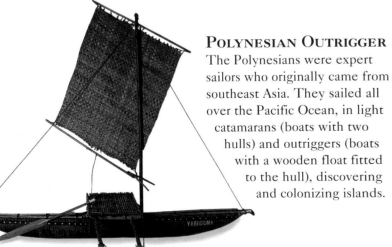

REED BOAT
Where there was no timber, people made boats from other materials. This reed boat is from Lake Titicaca, high in the Andes mountains of South America, where trees do not grow.

BIRCHBARK CANOE
Some people made canoes and boats by constructing a wooden frame and stretching animal hides or strips of bark over it to make light, waterproof craft. This birchbark canoe was made by the Algonquin—a Native American tribe from Ontario, Canada.

POLYNESIAN OUTRIGGER
The Polynesians were expert sailors who originally came from southeast Asia. They sailed all over the Pacific Ocean, in light catamarans (boats with two hulls) and outriggers (boats with a wooden float fitted to the hull), discovering and colonizing islands.

EGYPTIAN SHIP
From c. 3000 B.C.E., the Egyptians used imported wood to build strong seagoing ships with sails and oars for rowing and steering.

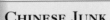

DOVER BOAT
Remains of a boat from c. 1500 B.C.E. shows early boats were built with planks in Northern Europe, as well as in the Mediterranean.

ROMAN TRADER
Roman trading ships sailed all around the Empire. This big barge, dating from c. 200 C.E., was used to bring grain from Egypt to Rome.

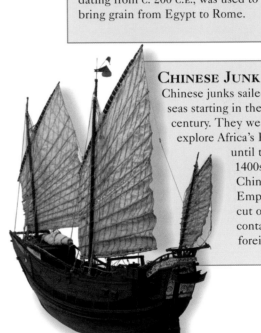

CHINESE JUNK
Chinese junks sailed the seas starting in the 5th or 6th century. They were used to explore Africa's East Coast until the early 1400s, when Chinese Emperors cut off all contact with foreigners.

VIKING KNORR
This Viking trader dates from the 11th century and was wider than a longship. The nautical term "starboard" comes from the steering oar or "steerboard," which was always on the right-hand side.

VENETIAN GALLEY
From around 1200 until 1700, countries around the Mediterranean favored galleys for both trading and military purposes. This painting shows Venetian war galleys.

Egyptian Ship

A TIMELINE OF SHIPPING

3000	2500	2000	1500

Dover Boat

GREEK TRADER
Greek galleys sailed the Mediterranean starting in c. 800 B.C.E. Traders usually had sails and one level of oars. Warships, such as the trireme, were powered by 170 oarsmen who sat in three levels.

ARAB DHOW
Since the 8th century, and probably earlier, Arab dhows with triangular lateen sails have crossed the Red Sea, Indian Ocean, and Persian Gulf, trading goods between continents.

COG
This 14th-century vessel from Northern Europe had a square sail and a central rudder, which became standard in all oceangoing ships.

CARAVEL
In the 15th century, the Portuguese sailed caravels in their search for a passage around Africa to India. Two of the ships Columbus used to sail to America in 1492 were caravels.

EAST INDIAMAN
The largest ships of the 18th and 19th centuries, East Indiamen carried passengers and cargo, but could also fight. Dividing the sails into several smaller ones meant they could be handled by a smaller crew.

PASSENGER LINER
From the late 19th century to the 1930s, shipping companies competed to produce the fastest, most luxurious liners. In 1906, the *Mauretania*, above, was the star liner of the Cunard Line.

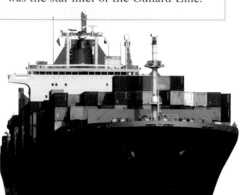

CONTAINER SHIP
Since the 1950s, much of the world's cargo has been transported in standard-size containers, which can be lifted on and off giant ships and trucks by cranes.

CLIPPER
The fastest sailing ships of the mid-19th century were the clippers that raced to China and back bringing tea to Europe. With its large sail area and narrow hull, a clipper could cover 310 miles (500 km) in a day.

OIL TANKER
In the 1950s and 60s, ever-larger oil tankers were designed to meet the growing demand for oil. The largest tankers today are often more than 1,476 ft (450 m) long.

CARRACK
The carrack of the 15th century was an important advance in ship design. Square sails and three masts gave it maneuverability. It also had raised constructions, called castles, at the front and back.

Greek Trader | | 500 | B.C.E. 0 | C.E. 100 | Roman Trader 200 | 300 | Chinese Junk 400 | 500 | 600 | Arab Dhow 700 | 800 | 900 | Viking Knorr 1000 | 1100 | Venetian Galley 1200 | Cog 1300 | Caravel 1400 | Carrack | Galleon 1500 | 1600 | 1700 | East Indiaman | Clipper 1800 | Steamship | 1900 | Passenger Liner | Oil tanker | Container Ship 2000 | *Queen Mary 2*

GALLEON
Developed from the carrack, a galleon was a square-sailed, three-masted sailing ship that sailed the seas from the 16th to 17th centuries. It could be a formidable fighting ship and was particularly popular with the Spanish navy.

STEAMSHIP
In the 19th century, the introduction of steam power and the use of iron changed the design of trading and fighting ships. In 1838, the *Great Western* (right) was the first ship to cross the Atlantic using steam power.

QUEEN MARY 2
As cruise holidays become ever more popular, shipping companies are building new, bigger liners. The *Queen Mary 2*, launched in 2004, can carry 2,620 passengers and 1,253 crew.

WHERE IS HE?

Did you spot the accident-prone characters in red, yellow, and green getting into trouble over the centuries? Check below that you found the right man.

PAGES 4-5
He's caught a crab ... is chasing a goose ... is stubbing his toe ... is falling off the quay.

PAGE 6
He's knocked over a pile of ivory.

PAGE 8
A goat has spotted him behind the jewelry smith.

PAGE 11
He's getting a beating outside the inn.

PAGE 12
The traveling dentist has him in his clutches.

PAGE 15
He's managed to get his foot stuck in a bucket.

PAGE 17
He's holding on tight at the top of the slave ship.

PAGE 18
He's the man who's feeling very seasick.

PAGE 21
Did you spot him under the table in the tavern?

PAGE 23
He's about to get doused with wet paint!

PAGE 25
He's managed to get caught up in a deckchair.

PAGE 27
He's in trouble again, this time with the police.

CREDITS

Index: Sylvia Potter
Maps: Ed Merrit

The publisher would like to thank the following for their kind permission to reproduce their photographs:

(Key: a-above; b-below/bottom; c-center; f-far; l-left; r-right; t-top)
akg-images: 30frb; Peter Connolly 30bc. **Alamy Images:** Kos Picture Source 31fcr; Peter Titmuss 31br. **The Art Archive:** Museo Correr Venice/Dagli Orti (A) 30fcr; Dagli Orti 30tc; Eileen Tweedy 31bc. The Trustees of the British Museum: 5ftl, 5tl; **Corbis:** 29fcla; Joel W. Rogers 31bl. **DK Images:**

Exeter Maritime Museum, The National Maritime Museum, London 30fcla, 30fcl, 30fttr; International Sailing Craft Association, Lowestoft 30bl; National Maritime Museum, London 29fcra, 30cr, 30fbr, 30br, 31clb, 31ftr, 31ftl; Wilberforce House Museum, Hull 29bc. **Dover Museum:** The Dover Bronze Age Boat Trust 30c. **Getty Images:** Workbook Stock 31cr. **Michael Holford:** 30tr. **Mary Evans Picture Library:** 31fcl. **National Maritime Museum, London:** 29tr, 31cla.

All other images © Dorling Kindersley
For further information see: www.dkimages.com